DC PHOTO BOOK

An Insider's View of Washington, DC

PHOTOGRAPHY BY STEPHEN R. BROWN

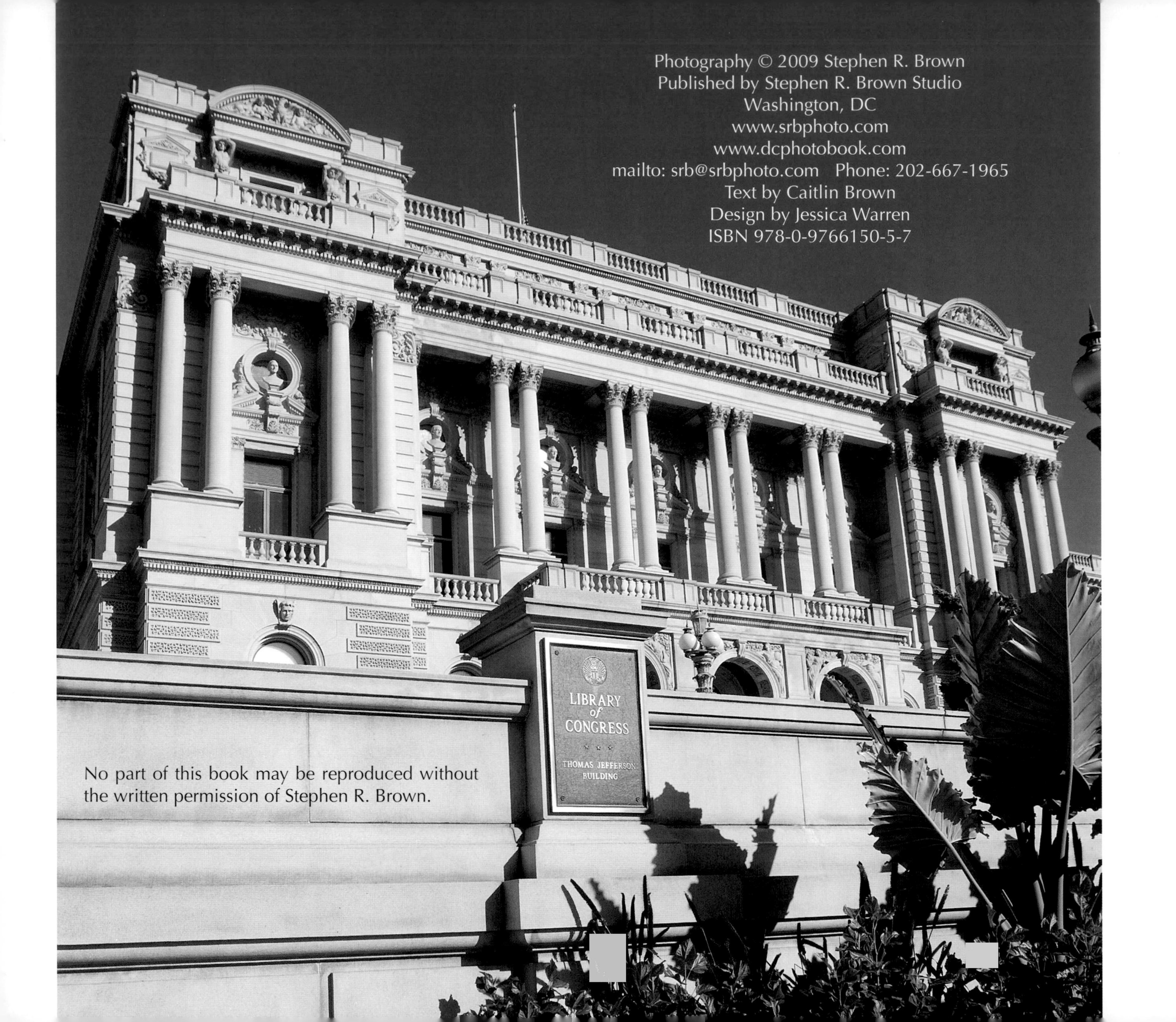

Published by Stephen R. Brown Studio
Washington, DC
www.srbphoto.com
www.dcphotobook.com
mailto: srb@srbphoto.com Phone: 202-667-1965
Text by Caitlin Brown
Design by Jessica Warren
ISBN 978-0-9766150-5-7

CONTENTS:

INTRODUCTION

Washington DC is a photographer's paradise. Its low-lying landscape is dictated by the highest building in town—the Washington Monument. The publicly funded architecture is wonderfully ornate, and thanks to the abundance of sky and light, the ever-changing shadow and color make for endlessly interesting views. If the drivers of DC are as bad as rumored, it's simply because the scenery is so extraordinary. I always have a camera when I cruise the city and many of these photographs were taken on these drives. I often will go back to the same place to get a satisfactory view.

Many of the Insider's Views images were taken on assignment for some of the world's major magazines and papers - *Smithsonian, Life, Time, Newsweek, U.S. News and World Report* and *The Washington Post*. All have headquarters or offices right here in the District. As a frequent contributor to these publications and a member of the White House News Photographers Association and the United States Senate Gallery, I have had the opportunity to wander and explore where most citizens cannot. I am also a "friend" of the Guild of Professional Tour Guides of Washington, DC and to my fellow DC enthusiasts, I admit this book is but a cursory glance. This city is a stimulating environment and an amazing place to live, work and photograph.

My daughter Caitlin (text and design), my wife June (editing), and Jessica Warren (design) worked with me to put the book together. Ellen Gold, past President of the Guild of Professional Guides gave the book several readings for historical and factual accuracy. Mary Pettinato of Honor Flight Chicago and Jeffrey Wilkes of This Old School were also kind enough to read the manuscript through. If there are remaining errors, they are mine. Jeff Tinsley of Smithsonian provided the Mall aerials, and Pete Souza and Chuck Kennedy, President Obama's personal photographers, provided the pictures on pages 44-45.

PART I:
THE NATIONAL MALL AND ENVIRONS

THE UNITED STATES SUPREME COURT

On a chilly day in December 1998, Native American rights activists gathered at the steps of the Supreme Court, taking a physical stance to express their opinions on the case that would be argued that morning, Minnesota v. Mille Lacs Band of Chippewa Indians. To DC natives, such a demonstration, though unique in content, is a relatively common occurrence. From the Jay Court to the present, Americans have brought their political views to the foot of the building around which our justice system revolves. The Supreme Court building, erected in 1935, has since been designated a National Historic Landmark.

Historians often discuss the Supreme Court according to who was Chief Justice at the time, as the nature of the court's decisions depends hugely on the views of its nine members.

EQUAL JUSTICE UNDER LAW

EQUAL·JUSTICE·UNDER·LAW

THE UNITED STATES CAPITOL

Sitting on the West Steps of the Capitol during summer concerts, DC residents and visitors often stare, enchanted, at the stunning model of American Neoclassic architecture that towers above them. The building's exterior size and soaring dome proclaim its importance. For through those columns lies a forum in which the world's most influential leaders have debated and formed the decisions that shape our country and our world; The Senate occupies the Capitol's north wing, and the House of Representatives occupies the south. The Eastern Front overlooks a newly renovated entrance that has and will serve as the traditional entrance for visiting dignitaries. The building's interior abounds with art depicting various historic figures and symbols of the United States.

The importance of the Capitol is evident not only in its political implications but also in its geographic ones, as the building's location on Capitol Hill intersects the four quadrants of the city.

AN INSIDER'S VIEW

THE INAUGURATION. On January 20, 1981, Ronald Reagan broke tradition and changed history, taking the oath of office on the terrace of the Capitol's West Front (top left). The day celebrated the victorious election for the Republicans in both the White House and the Senate, as well as the Iranian rebels' release of American hostages. In his inaugural address, however, Reagan reminded the American people, "To a few of us here today, this is a solemn and most momentous occasion; and yet, in the history of our Nation, it is a commonplace occurrence. The orderly transfer of authority as called for in the Constitution routinely takes place as it has for almost two centuries and few of us stop to think how unique we really are."

How better, then, to capture the distinctiveness of the Americans who gathered on the National Mall on that surprisingly mild January morning than through an equally unique photograph? The National Park Service helicopter is the only aircraft allowed to fly over the Mall on Inauguration Day, so aerial images of the Presidential Inauguration and ceremonies are coveted by photographers. The exclusivity of this image, taken from a National Park Service helicopter, for *Life Magazine* lies in the view. Only through an aerial view like this can a photographer capture the full effect of the sea of Americans gathered for a celebration of such historical import.

"Standing here," remarked Reagan in closing, "one faces a magnificent vista, opening up on this city's special beauty and history. At the end of this open mall are those shrines to the giants on whose shoulders we stand."

And so, later in Reagan's presidency, there was another momentous occasion on the Mall (bottom left). This time, however, the people gathered at the base of the Capitol were protestors calling for a larger voice for women and women's equality.

THE NATIONAL GALLERY OF ART

Whoever advised against judging a book by its cover had clearly never seen the National Gallery of Art, whose two buildings have distinctive exteriors that represent the diverse collections housed within. The newer East Wing, whose modern exterior is shown in these photographs, was designed by I.M.Pei and completed in 1978 to house a collection of contemporary art. The East Wing serves as an addition to

the original West Wing, founded in 1937 by Andrew Mellon to showcase American and European Art of different media from the 12th to 20th centuries.

The gallery was created by a joint resolution of Congress and opened to the public in 1941, after Mellon's death. It contains more than 2,000 pieces.

THE NATIONAL MUSEUM OF THE AMERICAN INDIAN

Since its opening in 2004, the Smithsonian's National Museum of the American Indian has surely captured the eye of every visitor to the National Mall. The building's yellow Kasota limestone exterior and nonlinear shape provide a stark contrast to the

traditional structures in its vicinity. Inside, the lack of sharp corners emphasizes the center's organic fluidity, which reflects the Native American concept of unity with the environment. Many of the museum's employees are of Native American descent.

PENNSYLVANIA AVENUE

The traditional path for parades and protests, the route of the inaugural march for every president since Jefferson, Pennsylvania Avenue connects the United States Capitol and the White House. Although the street extends over 35 miles through the city and beyond, the 1.2-mile stretch between the two landmarks marks the root of its fame. Pennsylvania Avenue is home to the Newseum (below) and is adjacent to the West Wing of the National Gallery of Art (far right), both of which have clear views of the nearby Capitol building. The Navy Memorial (right) and the Reagan Building (below, right) are also avenue landmarks.

Famous marches down Pennsylvania Avenue include a parade for women's suffrage led by activist Alice Paul and a march for unemployment aid during the 1890s depression led by Jacob Coxey.

NATIONAL GALLERY OF ART

ARCHIVES OF THE UNITED STATES OF AMERICA
Charters of Freedom
Declaration of Independence
Constitution
Bill of Rights
RUNNING FOR OFFICE
Candidates, Campaigns, and the Cartoons of Clifford Berryman
Gallery
THE NATIONAL ARCHIVES EXPERIENCE
Public Vaults
William G. McGowan Theater
Boeing Learning Center
Girl Scout Council
of the
Nation's Capital
Girl Scouts

THE NATIONAL ARCHIVES

"This building holds in trust the records of our national life and symbolizes our faith in the permanency of our national institutions." These words, engraved on the east side of the National Archives Building, capture perfectly the symbolic and practical nature of its role. Inside the elegant columns and bronze doors of the building lie the three most important documents in the establishment of the United States: the Declaration of Independence, the Constitution, and the Bill of Rights. Also housed in the archives is the Magna Carta, which dates to 1297. Together, these four documents are displayed in the Rotunda for the Charters of Freedom, the main chamber open to visitors.

The building's permanent exhibit is known as the Public Vaults, and contains at any given time about 1100 records in documents, drawings, films, maps and sound recordings. Exhibits feature outside collections, which visitors often visit in concurrence with one of the building's lecture or film series.

AN INSIDER'S VIEW

THE UPKEEP. Preservation is one of the most important tasks performed within the walls of the National Archives Building, as protection and conservation of important documents such as the Declaration of Independence is key.

Visitors to the Rotunda view the documents through hardened glass. In this rare photograph taken before the Archives were renovated, you can see that the documents were raised for viewing during the day and then lowered back into an allegedly "nuclear proof" vault at night for safe keeping. In an emergency, the documents couild be lowered from their viewing position in the Atrium above into the steel case and giant steel doors closed over the documents. In our current security situation, the Archives will not reveal their new methods of securing the documents after viewing hours.

The Declaration of Independence, the Constitution, and the Bill of Rights have occupied the space in the Rotunda since 1952. Officials placed the documents into airtight encasements filled with inert argon gases, a protective measure designed to preserve the documents in perpetuity. Conservators perform routine checks of the documents and the cases that hold them. Recent electronic advances have augmented these inspections.

UNITED STATES OF AMERICA
G
EXHIBIT

THE SCULPTURE GARDEN

The majestic blue bristles of Claes Oldenburg's typewriter eraser are visible from every corner of the National Gallery of Art Sculpture Garden, reminding visitors that not every statue in this capital city follows the conventional, historic mold. Oldenburg's modern piece stands among the works of Miró, Calder, and others whose collective artistic effort provides a refreshing break from the traditional buildings and sculptures that dominate the National Mall.

Completed in 1999, the Sculpture Garden boasts 17 major works of contemporary art. At its center lies a large fountain, the site for the Jazz in the Garden summer concert series. In the winter, the fountain is converted into a skating rink (left), making the garden a popular spot for visitors year round.

THE NATIONAL AIR AND SPACE MUSEUM

The most popular of the Smithsonian museums, this building houses the world's largest collection of historic air and spacecraft. Notable displays include the Apollo 11 command module, the Spirit of St. Louis, the Wright Flyer, and a moon rock from the Apollo 17 mission.

Originally called the National Air Museum, the building was renamed to include the extraterrestrial after the huge advances made during the Space Race of the 1960s. In fact, visitors learn specifically about the competition between the United States and the Soviet Union in an exhibition called *Space Race*.

Visitors to the museum also have access to 21 other exhibition galleries, an Imax theater, flight simulators, and a café. Additionally, the museum's Udvar-Hazy Center near Dulles Airport houses and displays more of the collection, which quickly exceeded the spatial limitations of the National Mall facility. Most museums maintain facilities outside the city to store their excess treasure.

U.S. MAIL
CAM-1
FLY-EASTERN AIR LINES
EASTERN
DOUGLAS
DC-3
1936
Entered Service
FORD
5-AT TRI-MOTOR
1928
Entered Service
TWA
247-D

THE HIRSHHORN MUSEUM

Before entering the building, the four-acre, two-level Sculpture Garden at the Hirshhorn Museum, teeming with contemporary sculptures (Rodin's distorted, bronze figures and di Suervo's minimalist industrial creations, among others), provides the visitor with a glimpse into the nature of the 11,500 pieces at the museum. The museum's ultra-modern exterior is no coincidence—architect Gordon Bunshaft intended for his design to stand out among the traditional structures on the National Mall, as he knew the artwork within its walls would be anything but conventional.

Opened in 1974, the Hirshhorn is the first museum in the District devoted solely to contemporary art, focusing with particular emphasis on art from the last quarter of the 21st century through the present. Though critics consider its collection of 19th and 20th century sculpture to be its strongest aspect, the museum also lays claim to many modern masterpieces in painting, including works by Richter, Bacon, and Man Ray.

THE CASTLE

The Smithsonian Castle was designed by architect James Renwick, Jr. in 1847 and as the first building on the Mall was meant to be the focal point of the Mall. It is bordered on the East by the Arts and Industries Building and on the West by the Freer Gallery of Art and the Museum of African Art.

An extensive series of gardens and walkways surround and link the museums which also border on Independence Avenue which runs east to west and attracts heavy traffic throughout the week. It is normally the route the Presidential motorcade takes on the way to the Capitol.

Ironically, the Smithsonian Institution was the result of a will left by James Smithson, a British scientist who never visited the United States. It has been suggested that his bequest was made because of his Enlightenment ideals of democracy and education which he felt would be best fulfilled in America.

THE WASHINGTON MONUMENT

Staring up at the marble clad obelisk, you will notice a slight color change that begins about 150 feet from the monument's base and wonder if this was part of architect Robert Mills' master plan. Construction of the monument intended to honor George Washington began in 1848. In fact, the gradient line marks the height at which construction was stopped in 1854 due to a lack of funding; the darker color of the top two thirds is due to the inability to use the exact same stone as the original when construction resumed in 1879.

Apart from its color, the Washington Monument carries other hues of intrigue, one of which is its height. Reaching 555 feet into the DC skyline, the structure towers over much of the District's low-lying landscape. Many residents believe that no building in the city can legally be taller than the Washington Monument, when, in reality, there exists no such law. This popular misconception only serves to underscore the significance of the monument, a tribute to our founding fathers and the values upon which this country stands.

The Washington Monument is not only a powerful icon but also an ever-present one. As one enters the District, be it by car or by train, by land or air or sea, the obelisk is often the very first glimpse of the hub so rich in history. Children know it from an early age as "The Giant Pencil" and learn that the monument stands as a constant reminder of a leader who set a precedent and embodied the tenets of democracy that define our nation today. Even its reflection in the Reflecting Pool (left), which extends to the Lincoln Memorial, proves an icon of elegance and grace.

The monument was completed in 1884 and opened to the public in 1888 after finalization of the interior. After the years of debate and struggle for continued funding in Congress, the structure's total cost came to just over a million dollars. At one time visitors could climb the breathtaking 897 stairs to reach the top. Today, the elevator is the only option offered without a special permit.

Either way, the view is well worth the ascent.

AN INSIDER'S VIEW

THE LOST PERSPECTIVE. As the security measures on the National Mall increase, access to the best vantage points, such as the rooftops of monuments and memorials, becomes a near impossibility. Taken in 1981, this photograph captures the Independence Day fireworks with the Capitol and the Washington Monument aligned in the background, the Washington Monument elegantly mirrored in the Reflecting Pool. How did the photographer achieve this viewpoint, one so unattainable today? Before security heightened, the government granted certain photographers access to the roof of the Lincoln Memorial so they could document the fireworks from this breathtaking perspective.

For many photographers, a successful fireworks photograph is marked by one or more distinctive reference points, such as a monument or official building. On the National Mall, however, this is becoming an increasingly difficult objective; many photographers wonder whether shots like this one will become obsolete if security trends continue to heighten. The White House News Photographers Association was formed so photographers could present a united front to White House officials, the five police forces in DC and bureaucrats who were preventing First Amendment access to these treasured views.

THE WHITE HOUSE

It is more exclusive than DC's hottest nightclubs, with a reservation waiting list longer than those of top restaurants. Despite this, 1600 Pennsylvania Avenue still receives thousands of visitors a day. At this home of the first family and workplace of the president, security is tight, but once a visitor enters the House he or she has the chance to view several of the 132 rooms of different designs and themes.

John Adams was the first president to live in the White House, moving in shortly after its construction was completed in 1800. The original design, submitted by James Hoban, was chosen in a contest with nine submissions, including an anonymous one by Thomas Jefferson. Today, the mansion consists of the Executive Residence, East Wing, and West Wing, where the President's Oval Office is located. The White House also boasts many recreational facilities and is equipped for great parties. The recent pictures of President Obama were taken by Pete Souza, the official photographer of the President who is with him day and night.

The South Lawn of the White House is a great place for a party. Photo by Pete Souza

The Presidential helicopter is the only helicopter to land on the White House lawn. Photo by Chuck Kennedy

President Obama returns with hamburgers for the staff. Photo by Pete Souza

President Obama escorts former First Lady Nancy Reagan. Photo by Pete Souza

President Reagan and wife Nancy head for Camp David, the Presidential Retreat. Photo © 1984 Stephen R. Brown

THE NATIONAL WORLD WAR II MEMORIAL

On May 29, 2004, thousands of people gathered on the Mall for the dedication of the National World War II Memorial, established to honor the 16 million men and women who served the United States during the war. The memorial took three years to complete and was funded primarily by private contributors; the federal government only provided $16 million of the $197 million accumulated to build and maintain the site.

Architect Friedrich St. Florian's idea for the memorial, featuring a semicircular array of engraved pillars and a wall of gold stars, won a nationwide design contest out of over 400 submissions. The memorial features twenty-four bas-reliefs depicting wartime scenes, and two clusters of four eagles all created by sculptor Raymond Kaskey.

Today, the memorial is a popular site for veterans and families, attracting over 4 million visitors a year. Honor Flight, a nonprofit organization, works to fly veterans from across the country for free to see their memorial, cognizant of the fact that as of 2010, 1,200 World War II veterans pass away daily. Senator Robert Dole usually greets them several days a week.

PACIFIC
PACIFIC
WAR II MEMORIAL

ATLANTIC
WORLD WAR II MEMORIAL

AN INSIDER'S VIEW

THE CONTROVERSY. In 1994, President Clinton signed a resolution stating that the World War II Memorial must be located on the National Mall, despite limited space and the danger of interrupting an area of utmost historic import. Officials considered three sites, ultimately selecting the Rainbow Pool. The decision, made public on October 5, 1995, sparked immediate controversy.

Located directly between the Lincoln Memorial and the Washington Monument, the Rainbow Pool site historically allowed for an unbroken view between the two landmarks; construction of a memorial around it would obstruct the line of sight. Furthermore, the space near the reflecting pool and Constitution Gardens is a historic site for demonstrations and marches. If a World War II Memorial had existed in 1963, critics pondered, would there have been room for the 250,000 people who marched on the Rainbow Pool site to hear Martin Luther King's "I Have a Dream" speech? Despite such misgivings, the construction process not only continued, but was expedited due to the fact that World War II veterans were dying and an adequate memorial was yet to be built. Congress passed legislation that exempted the memorial from further review and dismissed legal challenges to the memorial, curtailing the normally lengthy approval process.

In response, critics formed the National Coalition to Save Our Mall. In the introduction to a January 2000 web article entitled "The World War II Memorial Defaces a National Treasure," the coalition of critics and veterans asserted that the memorial "drives a wedge between the Washington Monument and the Lincoln Memorial, breaking the connection between the nation's two most prominent symbols of democracy."

Today, the Memorial columns are 20 feet lower than the original design and it is the most-visited memorial in the city. Now the columns frame rather than block the views.

to right by Jeff Tinsley, Smithsonian.

THE TIDAL BASIN AND CHERRY BLOSSOMS

The inauguration of President Barack Obama attracted over a million people to the National Mall, but there is an annual celebration that draws in a crowd to rival this historic attendance record: The National Cherry Blossom Festival. Tourists come from all over the world to the District each spring to view the trees in their short, two-week blooming period. The festival is in commemoration of the Mayor of Tokyo's 1932 gift of 3,000 trees to the United States to strengthen the growing diplomatic relationship between the U.S. and Japan.

The cherry blossom trees line the Tidal Basin, the man-made inlet that functions to regulate the water levels of the Washington Channel, storing the overflow from high tide.

The basin was dredged in the late 19th century. Today, the elegance of the Tidal Basin attracts many visitors. A sight sure to put a smile on every face is that of hundreds of paddleboats meandering along the surface in the summer, gliding across the reflections of the Jefferson Memorial.

THE THOMAS JEFFERSON MEMORIAL

Author of the Declaration of Independence and third president of the United States, Thomas Jefferson was a man of great ideas. Fitting, then, is the monument erected in his memory, whose exterior recalls that of the Pantheon and whose interior boasts excerpts from Jefferson's letters and other sources, including the Declaration of Independence.

Designed by architect John Russell Pope and dedicated in 1943, the memorial drew criticism even during its construction. Today, however, the structure is widely celebrated as a cornerstone of the National Mall and attracts countless visitors, especially during the annual National Cherry Blossom Festival.

Rudolph Evans' bronze statue of Jefferson (left), added four years after dedication, stands proudly in the center of the dome.

THEY (WHO) SEEK TO ESTABLISH
SYSTEMS OF GOVERNMENT BASED ON
THE REGIMENTATION OF ALL HUMAN
BEINGS BY A HANDFUL OF INDIVIDUAL
RULERS... CALL THIS A NEW ORDER.
IT IS NOT NEW AND IT IS NOT ORDER.

THE FDR MEMORIAL

"Physical strength," spoke President Franklin Delano Roosevelt, "can never permanently withstand the impact of spiritual force." This statement certainly reflects the man's lifelong struggle with paralytic illness, a condition that he refused to accept to the end of his days. Whether truly optimistic or in denial, FDR almost never appeared in public in his wheelchair; consequently, the appearance of the President both in his chair and standing upright in the memorial design led to major controversy.

Dedicated in 1997, the memorial consists of four "rooms" that progress through the 12 years of FDR's presidency. Water plays a symbolic role throughout the monument, representing "The Great Depression", World War II, and other major events of the era.

THE VIETNAM VETERANS MEMORIAL

Often referred to simply as "The Wall," the Vietnam Veterans Memorial stands to honor the millions of men and women who served in the Vietnam War. The memorial is two walls totalling 493.5 feet that list over 58,000 names of dead or missing members of the US armed forces. The original design called for a memorial harmonious with its surroundings; the black, reflective surface of the walls gives the memorial a mirror-like quality, and the walls point toward the Washington Monument in one direction and the Lincoln Memorial in the other, grounding the names in history.

Creating a memorial for the most controversial war in US history was, naturally, a contentiious process. The memorial fund stipulated that the commemorative structure must focus not on the war but on those who lost their lives fighting it. Still, controversy arose over Yale architecture student Maya Lin's nontraditional design; consequently, Frederick Hart was appointed to create a more traditional bronze sculpture nearby. Hart's "Three Soldiers" stands near the wall, featuring three members of the armed forces who appear exhausted from combat. The Women's Memorial was erected to honor the women who served in the war, many of whom were nurses.

Today, visitors often leave commemorative gifts at the foot of the wall near the name of a friend or relative. The National Park Service collects and stores goods left at the memorial.

AN INSIDER'S VIEW

THE DEDICATION. In 1979, a group of Vietnam veterans founded the Vietnam Veterans Memorial Fund (VVMF), an organization that worked towards a national tribute for Americans who served the U.S. in the Vietnam War. On November 13, 1982 their goal became a reality, as that day marked the dedication of the Vietnam Veterans Memorial.

As 150,000 people flocked to the National Mall to participate in the dedication ceremony, members of the VVMF surely felt a surge of pride in the overwhelming support for their objective, despite the controversy that surrounded Maya Lin's design for the memorial during its construction. Thousands of veterans and supporters paraded down Constitution Avenue toward the Wall, some wearing old clothes worn in battle and others clad in bright, celebratory colors. Many members of the crowd had actually opposed the war, but, that day, marched along to honor those who risked their lives to fight in it.

After ceremonial speeches and singing, veteran Jan C. Scruggs formally dedicated the memorial. The hundreds of thousands who had gathered on the Mall dashed to find the names of their lost loved ones on the Wall; hands reached out in every direction and continued to search well into the night. National Park Service volunteers and rangers help visitors locate and make pencil etchings of their loved ones' names on the Wall.

THE LINCOLN MEMORIAL

At 6'4", Abraham Lincoln was the tallest president to date. The stone statue of Lincoln, however, would tower over the original at an astounding 28 feet tall (if he stood up from that giant stone chair). Daniel Chester French's sculpture of the 16th president sits inside a structure in the style of a Greek Doric temple, designed by architect Henry Bacon.

Built in 1922, the Lincoln Memorial honors the leader whose ideas moved and reunited a struggling nation. The inside walls display inscriptions of Lincoln's most famous speeches, the Gettysburg Address

and his second inaugural address. Martin Luther King, Jr., stood on the steps of the memorial to deliver his "I Have a Dream" speech in 1963, at the feet of the man whose presidency had lead to abolishing slavery 100 years earlier.

DISTRICT OF COLUMBIA WHO

MEMORIALS TUCKED AWAY

Around the National Mall lie smaller memorials which have been getting more attention as the city grows in popularity. The DC War Memorial (far left) on the National Mall serves to commemorate the 26,000 citizens of the District of Columbia who served in World War I. It is scheduled for renovation and calls have been made for renaming it the "World War I Memorial".

The U.S. Air Force Memorial, located near the Pentagon and overlooking the city, honors Air Force personnel through three soaring, stainless steel spires that evoke the contrails of the Air Force Thunderbirds. The Korean War Veterans Memorial consists of 19 statues of soldiers dressed in full combat gear in the rugged Korean terrain.

PART II:
ARLINGTON, VA

THE WOMEN IN MILITARY SERVICE FOR AMERICA MEMORIAL

Dedicated in 1997, this memorial stands at one entrance to Arlington National Cemetery. The Women's Memorial is the first and, to date, only commemorative edifice of its kind, honoring all women who have served the United States since the American Revolution.

Structurally, the memorial mixes tradition and modernity. The outside of the building, designed by architects Marion Weiss and Michael Manfredi, blends subtly into the elegant hillside with its stone plaza, tall arches, and dark reflecting pool. Additionally, large glass tablets stand against the wall, understated but powerful in their engravings about the experiences of different servicewomen.

Inside visitors encounter the magnificent skylit museum area, which houses permanent collections and seasonal exhibits that document the history of women in the military. The growing library and compilation of photographs, documents, and personal artifacts provide a rich addition to the surrounding military culture.

ARLINGTON NATIONAL CEMETERY

Arlington House sits high above a sea of tombstones. Prior to the Civil War, it was the mansion of Confederate General Robert E. Lee. During the Civil War, Union General Montgomery Meigs ordered that Union soldiers be buried in Lee's front yard, in part to prevent Lee, considered a traitor, from ever returning to the property again.

Today, the house serves as a memorial and sign of respect for General Lee, and those first 26 Union soldiers buried on the property mark the beginning of Arlington National Cemetery. The vast graveyard is the burial site of more than 300,000 military veterans and public figures, from the American Revolution to the present. Notable gravesites include Pierre L'Enfant, Thurgood Marshall, the crew of the Challenger Space Shuttle, William Howard Taft, and President John Kennedy and his brothers, Senators Robert and Ted.

One of the most visited areas of the cemetery is the Tomb of the Unknowns, which overlooks the District from a hill as a reminder of the importance of every individual who serves this nation.

MINOW
JORDAN
SHEPARD
OECHSLIN

AN INSIDER'S VIEW

INTERMENT. A beacon of honor and patriotism, Arlington National Cemetery is a an ever-expanding burial site for those who have served the United States. Due to limited space, however, the cemetery maintains the most restrictive criteria of all national burial grounds. Although the conditions for burial in Arlington National Cemetery are extensive and strict, the burial site still averages around 28 funerals per day.

Funeral proceedings at the cemetery are traditional, often rooted in historic ritual for dealing with comrades fallen in battle. The casket is draped with the American flag, recalling the custom of covering the dead carried from the battlefield that began during the Napoleonic Wars. When riflemen fire three rifle volleys over the grave, they echo the indicator used to halt fighting to remove the dead from the battlefield.

Perhaps the most famous funereal practice at Arlington Cemetery is the 21-Gun Salute, also known as the Presidential Salute. Cannon salutes, symbolizing trust and reverence, originated in the British Navy; a battleship would fire its cannons out to sea to empty its ammunition and signify its peaceful intent. Normally a bugler plays taps at the end of a ceremony. The photographs to the left depict the funeral for Robert Tills, an ensign whose death marked the first casualty of WWII. His PBY was lost to the Japanese fleet flying to attack Pearl Harbor. While his loss was well-known and a destroyer named after him, his remains were only recently recovered in the hull of PBY #4 and he was buried in 2009, almost 70 years after his death to full military honors.

THE MARINE CORPS WAR MEMORIAL

While the dedication of this memorial is to all Marines who have died in defense of the United States, the statue is commonly known as the Iwo Jima Memorial, as it depicts the famous moment from World War II. The successful takeover of the island eventually led to the end of the war in 1945. In fact, the inspiration for the memorial was Joe Rosenthal's Pulitzer Prize winning photograph of the inspirational American flag raising atop Mount Suribachi in Japan.

Designed by Horace Peaslee, the memorial was dedicated in 1954 by President Eisenhower. The bronze figures stand 32 feet tall and occupy the same positions as the men in Rosenthal's photograph, raising the cloth American flag that flies 24 hours a day.

The granite base of the statue contains the engraving, "In honor and memory of the men of the United States Marine Corps who have given their lives to their country since November 10, 1775." On the opposite side, it reads, "Uncommon valor was a common virtue." (Admiral Nimitz speaking of his men)

Located at the entrance to Arlington National Cemetery, the memorial overlooks the Potomac River.

ARLINGTON MEMORIAL BRIDGE

Dedicated in 1932, Memorial Bridge is both an aesthetic wonder and a symbol of unity. The bridge spans the Potomac River and connects two memorials representing the Union and the Confederacy, the Lincoln Memorial and Arlington House, respectively.

Rumor has it that the construction of the bridge, which had been delayed since its original planning two decades before, was prompted when President Warren G. Harding found himself caught in three hours of traffic on the way to the Tomb of the Unknowns in Arlington, VA. The neoclassical structure initially functioned as a drawbridge, opening to allow barges to pass up the Potomac to Georgetown; this feature was abandoned, however, with the later, upstream construction of the Theodore Roosevelt Bridge, which has no draw feature.

Designed by the prestigious architectural firm, McKim, Mead and White, the bridge spans 2,163 feet long, with nine arches over the river. Each arch features a bas-relief eagle, emphasizing the majesty of the bridge as a symbol for the reunited country. On the eastern end, two neoclassical equestrian statues flank the bridge. Its wide sidewalks make for a popular running and biking area.

PART III:
THE CANAL, THE RIVER AND THE WATERFRONT

THE C & O CANAL

Where the Chesapeake and Ohio Canal cuts through Georgetown, one can find the only mules in the District of Columbia. Though the canal ceased to be active in 1924, many visitors enjoy rides down the historic waterway on boats pulled by these hybrid creatures, guided by park rangers in costume. The tour boats can even be rented out for private use.

The canal spans the 184.5 miles from Washington, DC, to Cumberland, MD. Because of the over 600-foot topographical incline between the two places, builders constructed 74 locks along the way, each of which would raise a canal boat about 8 feet. In 1971 the canal became a National Historic Park, and today, the path alongside it is a popular trail for running, hiking, and biking. Popular areas along the canal include Glen Echo Park, the Billy Goat Trail, and Harper's Ferry.

WASHINGTON HARBOUR

From early spring to late autumn, early morning to late at night, the Georgetown waterfront bustles with activity. Overlooking the Potomac, the waterfront is perfect for viewing high school and college crew regattas as well as the countless people engaged in boating and water sports. Home to Thompson's Boat House, Washington Harbour attracts visitors looking to rent kayaks, small sailboats, sculls, and bikes.

The harbor also features several popular waterfront restaurants, as famous for their view as their food. Looking out at the Potomac River, diners see a series of majestic bridges and buildings such as the Kennedy Center and the Watergate complex. In the summer, the elegant fountain in the middle of the Washington Harbour restaurants draws adults and children alike to its steps, where musicians and street performers often showcase their talents.

SEQUOIA

THE KENNEDY CENTER

"I am certain," spoke President John F. Kennedy, "that after the dust of centuries has passed over our cities, we too, we will be remembered not for our victories or defeats in battle or politics, but for our contribution to the human spirit." How fitting, then, that this vibrant memorial for the revered president is a center for the arts, boasting plays, musicals, operas, dance and ballet, and music of all genres.

Located across from the Watergate complex, the Kennedy Center occupies a beautiful strip of land on the DC waterfront. The terrace overlooks the Potomac River, and audiences often step outside during intermission to find themselves as equally impressed by the scenic overlook as by the extraordinary performances inside the building's walls. Likewise, rowers have the landmark within sight from the river.

Opened in 1971, the Kennedy Center was designed by architect Edward Durrell Stone. Despite the extremely high cost, which grew from $10 million to $60 million during construction, critics from the media and national organizations alike supported the building. As a national memorial, the Kennedy Center receives federal funding, but its cultural and educational initiatives are paid for almost entirely by gifts and ticket sales.

202

PART IV: EXCURSIONS

DIESEL
BOOKS · OLSSON'S · RECORDS
RITZ CAMERA
YIELD

GEORGETOWN

Nestled above the Potomac River, Georgetown is one of the District's most vibrant neighborhoods. As one descends Wisconsin Avenue, the elegant townhouses give way to the myriad trendy shops and restaurants of M Street. The would-be college town boasts everything from chain stores and burger joints to upscale boutiques and restaurants and is, consequently, a favorite for shopping and dining.

Almost always busy, infallibly crowded to the point of bursting on Friday and Saturday nights, Georgetown features exciting nightlife. Just alongside the trendy bars and eateries, however, lie landmarks rooted in the rich history of this old tobacco port. Visitors to the neighborhood would be sorry to miss the historic house museums: Tudor Place, Dumbarton House, and the Old Stone House. Equally impressive are the gardens at Dumbarton House, on the property called Dumbarton Oaks. Indeed, the most appealing quality of Georgetown may be the wide variety of its attractions.

DUMBARTON OAKS

In 1944, representatives from the United States, the United Kingdom, the Soviet Union, and the Republic of China met at this Georgetown mansion for the historic Dumbarton Oaks Conference. Less than two months of negotiations produced what would become the most important international body: the United Nations.

Today, visitors to the Federal-style building spend hours strolling through the lavish gardens. The site is also a center for scholarship.

The adjoining neighborhood is known for its gorgeous houses and elaborate shrubbery (right).

THE WASHINGTON NATIONAL CATHEDRAL

This true European Gothic cathedral was built in the 20th Century. The National Cathedral presents an exterior to rival Notre Dame in Paris but just recently celebrated its 100th birthday. In fact, construction only finished in 1990 under President Bush.

Pierre L'Enfant's design for the city included a designated area for a house of worship for all people. The National Portrait Gallery, however, claimed that space, so the cathedral planning committee selected Mount Saint Alban as the new site. Visitors enjoy tours through the towers and music by the Cathedral Choir of Men and Girls, which includes girls from the National Cathedral School and boys from St. Alban's, both of which are located on the cathedral close.

DUPONT CIRCLE

Central to the "old city" as planned by Pierre L'Enfant, Dupont Circle is one of the most interesting and accessible neighborhoods in the District. It is one of DC's oldest and architecturally ornate neighborhoods. Many of the mansions built in the area in the 1870s have been preserved, and there is still a trolley station (though currently inaccessible) underneath the circle.

Chess players, tourists and families relax and play in Dupont Circle Park seemingly oblivious to the incredible traffic flowing by. Connecticut Avenue, one of the city's central arteries, runs directly underneath the circle through a tunnel constructed in 1949. On one side of the circle is Eastern Massachusetts Avenue, home to think-tanks. Opposite that is Western Massachusetts Avenue, noted for Embassy Row, which extends up to the Naval Observatory and Vice-Presidential mansion.

Like many Washington neighborhoods, Dupont Circle's scenery and location are iconic. The 1998 film "Enemy of the State" featured the circle and traffic tunnel. Furthermore, Presidential motorcades frequently pass through, as the President travels often to fundraisers at the hotels further north on Connecticut.

NATIONAL PORTRAIT GALLERY
SAAM
AMERICAN
SAAM
AMERICAN
SMITHSONIAN INSTITUTION
DONALD W. REYNOLDS CENTER FOR AMERICAN ART AND PORTRAITURE
NATIONAL PORTRAIT GALLERY
Museums open

NIGHT LIGHTS

While much of DC falls quiet at night, there are a number of neighborhoods and sites that come alive. Gallery Place and Chinatown (bottom right), home to the National Portrait Gallery and American Art Museum (opposite page), thrive when the sun sets. The streets of Adams Morgan (below) are packed on weekend evenings. The Main Avenue Fish Market (left) glows at night. And of course, the memorials, such as the Navy Memorial fountain (bottom left), are breathtaking when illuminated.

NATIONALS PARK

The first major "green" stadium in the United States, Nationals Park is a LEED-Certified structure. Nationals Park provides panoramic views of DC landmarks that rival the attractions of the stadium itself, as the Capitol and the Washington Monument are both visible from certain areas of its 41,888 seats. A recent addition to the DC waterfront, the stadium opened on March 30, 2008 when the Washington Nationals took on the Atlanta Braves. In MLB tradition, President Bush threw the first pitch, a ceremonial act that preceded a victorious opener.

SOUTHEAST DEVELOPMENT

Well into the 2000s, Southeast DC had little in the way of shopping, dining, and cultural attractions. In fact, city residents recognized the area for its consistently elevated crime rate and resulting tragic media reports, even in the section just below the U.S. Capitol. In 2005, however, construction of the new baseball stadium for the Washington Nationals began; with it came gradual changes in the landscape along the Southeast waterfront.

When the ballpark opened three years later, the surrounding area was virtually unrecognizable. The July 2007 demolition of parts of South Capitol Street had brought the area closer to sea level, and a newly painted, six-lane road had emerged. Developers had seized and replaced the nearby housing projects, shabby liquor stores, and rundown storage areas with new commercial structures.

Completion of the stadium, though, does not mean the end of development in Southeast. The city council and developers predict that the introduction of new office space, housing units, and retail stores will continue well into the next decade. The city is even building a water taxi pier at Diamond Teague Park, which would bring people across the Anacostia River to the southeast corner of the ballpark, and has plans to build another at The Yards, located several blocks east of the stadium. These services, residents anticipate, could be the first step in a water taxi system that would connect various points along the river, including Georgetown, National Harbor, and Alexandria.

"JUST ONE MORE": THE AWAKENING

In 1980, the National Park Service granted the Awakening sculpture a two-year permit, allowing the piece to reside in the district at Hains Point for the International Sculpture Conference Exhibition. The 100-foot giant emerging from the ground was so popular, however, that it remained there for almost 28 years, to the immense pleasure of visitors and residents.

When *LIFE Magazine* learned of the 1980 arrival, they commissioned photographer Stephen R. Brown to photograph the statue for a week. The magazine featured Brown's aerial image of the sculpture (right) on the last page, called "Just One More," reserved for premiere photographs.

As the image clearly depicts, the sculpture quickly became a playground for children and daring adults, or those willing to climb into the palm of a giant.

The picture on the far right is an outtake from the photo shoot. The lighting effects were made with a combination of strobes, car headlights and flashlights.

In 2007, sculptor J. Seward Johnson Jr. sold the Awakening to National Harbor, a new development on the DC waterfront. The sculpture was moved in 2008.

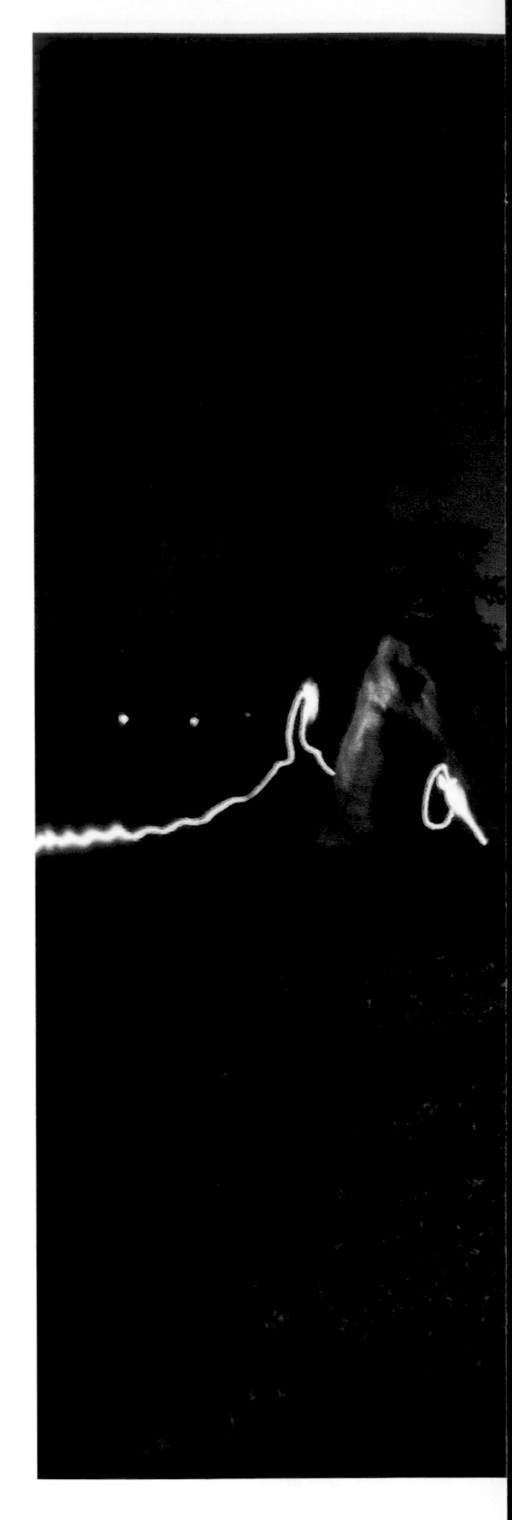

ON THE MOVE

Named after John Foster Dulles, Secretary of State under Eisenhower, Washington Dulles International Airport (left and right) is not the closest airport to the District but perhaps the most architecturally renowned. For shorter flights, residents choose the closer Ronald Reagan Washington National Airport (far right), which lies just across the bridge in Arlington, Virginia.

Union Station (below), the historic train station and shopping center, occupies a prominent site on Massachusetts Avenue, near the Capitol.

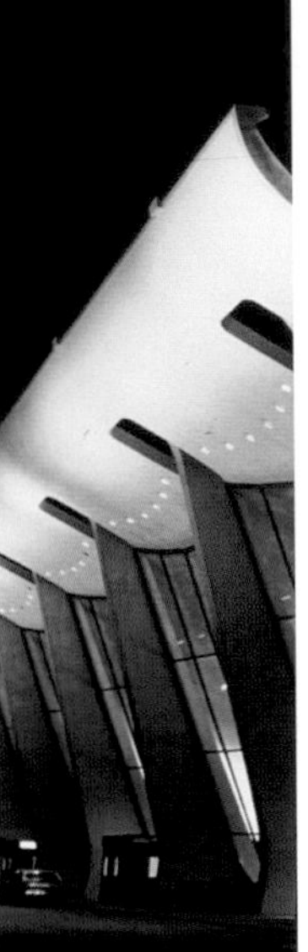

Ronald Reagan Washing
National Airport

WEST

Some vantage points require Presidential attention. I agreed to make a few pictures for Ronald Reagan's inaugural committee and asked for a letter signed by President Reagan requesting that the Capitol Police grant me access to the Dome at dawn. Name dropping works and they agreed. It was a cold morning and we rushed up the stairs to be there for the sunrise. As we emerged, the view was quite as spectacular as I had imagined and certainly worth the effort.

EAST

As you wander the National Mall there is always one magnificent view in front of you. And if you find yourself without a photograph, simply turn around. As you can see, it just gets better.

KILROY

And who was Kilroy? Rumors have it that he was an inspector in a Philadelphia ship building firm or that he worked in China as a maintenance engineer. This easily drawn cartoon became a symbol of quality control and American presence during WWII. There are many Kilroys who have claimed to be the "Real Kilroy" and there are several websites devoted to his legend. The designers of the WWII Memorial chose the Kilroy cartoon to symbolize the quality and care they put into building the memorial. You can find the cartoon at the entrance to the maintenance stairways at the WWII Memorial. Quite a few people have reported him to the Park Police as "graffiti." Welcome to Washington!